CROSSING THE BRIDGE

A comforting story about transition and letting go

Written and Illustrated
by
Lindsey Berkson

Introduction

Suzanne was my very first patient in junior clinic at The University of Western States 30 years ago. She was an angelic person, a passionate schoolteacher, who exuded sweetness and a real desire to be healthy. She was the ideal patient and did whatever she could to have vibrant health.

When I left Portland, Susan became a patient of a colleague of mine. Several years later, he developed cancer. Suzanne had known his wife earlier and soon she was there for both of them, by their sides for the length it took. She was there emotionally and spiritually, and she kept me abreast of every detail which I greatly appreciated. When I got breast cancer and when I was misdiagnosed with kidney cancer, she would regularly send me sweet little care packages. She didn't have much money but she gave great soul. She would send small satchels of tea for calming, simple sayings of encouragement, copies of speeches by revered holy people discussing hope or the victory of the human spirit.

Several years ago Suzanne was diagnosed with ovarian cancer. She had beaten it, and then it returned. One week I was driving down Anderson Lane and my cell phone rang. It was Suzanne but her voice was so low I had to pull the car over to the side of the road and get the window up to block out the street noise to hear her. She told me she needed me. She explained that she was dying and that even with all her spirituality and belief in God, she was ashamed to say that she was completely filled with fear. And, she admitted, this fear was ruining these last days with her beloved partner Dennis. She asked me to help her have less fear.

I asked if I could fly out there. She said their place was small and she was too tired. But would I think of something she could do, or think of?
Words? What could I say? Platitudes? No way. What could I do for this incredible being of light?

So I went to the gym and ran on the elliptical machine, where I do my best thinking. I prayed and

ran and asked the universe to help me help
Suzanne.

And suddenly I saw this book as clear as a path in
front of your feet. I jumped off the machine and
rushed home, writing and drawing as I was driving
down the road.

I FEDEXed the first draft of this book that night.
Dennis called me the next afternoon and said that
they had sat down and read it within 10 minutes.
Then they immediately started over and read it
again. By the end of the second read through,
Suzanne felt a peace she had not been able to
achieve before. The next week was filled with calm
and happiness.

I went on to draw a color version. And now, low and
behold, this work has held comfort, encouragement
and hope for quite a number of those on this
ultimate journey.

I hope this brings peace and gentleness to someone you love as well as yourself.

Lindsey Berkson

Austin, Texas

2010

Crossing the Bridge

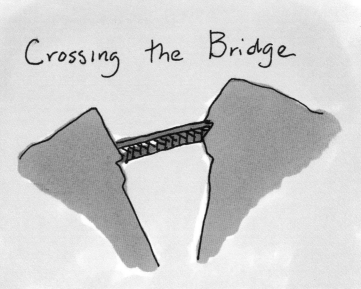

by

Lindsey Benkson

This was written and gifted
for Suzanne's crossing
But it has helped many
So now it's for you, too,

dying is a bridge...

...to another life.

Richard Alpert says...

`death is perfectly safe`

and I believe him.

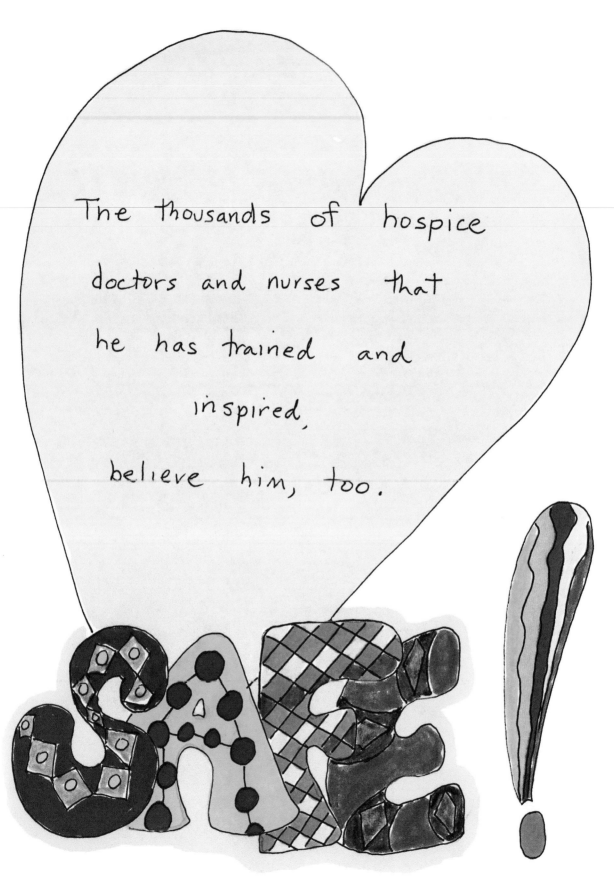

The thousands of hospice doctors and nurses that he has trained and inspired,

believe him, too.

SAGE!

with every cell, I believe.

Now that everything has been
done to keep you alive

But life as we know it
says it's time to let go

I honor your being here
And your <u>LETTING GO</u>!

Just as **FEAR**

is a natural part

of living,

It is a natural part

of crossing the bridge

But scoot fear off your bridge.

Don't let it _ruin_ your experience.

Suzanne,

You were my first patient in Junior Clinic. You got better. I felt hopeful. We shared

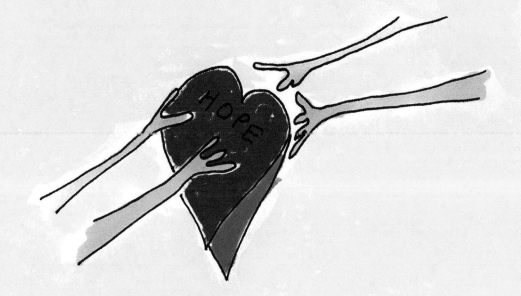

hope and struggle and joy and sorrow over these past 30 years.

Wherever you have walked,
Suzanne, you have

'seeded' HOPE!

Suzanne's path through life

I carry a Suzanne
hope tree,
rich with fruit,
in my heart♥

We have feasted

On your fruit

From your seeds.

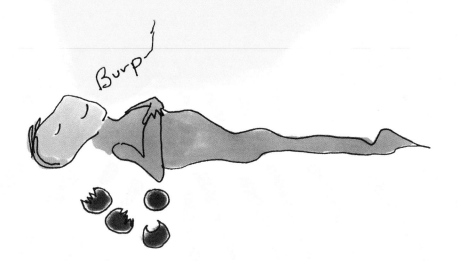

And now, because of
your cancer
You are <u>so</u> hungry!

life's sometimes
NOT FAIR!

death's sometimes
NOT FAIR!

But...

I know this with
every cell in my
body + heart

And you know how
much I have studied
science + religion, the
body + the mind, and
how often I have faced
death, myself.

So this is truth.

Dying is not an end.

It is a bridge...

...to more!

All those years and years
And skyscrapers of
words and passages
about divinity and God
and love...

THEY ARE REAL !!!

UP WITH GOD !!!

The French call love-making
the 'little death'.

Therapists call drug addiction
the 'slow death'.

But
Spiritually-in-the-know
   folks say death is
   how we molt,
   Like catepillars
           into butterflies.

We molt
and we
cross

the
bridge

To new life,
with God,
with loved ones,
and a
continued
journey.

But my prayers

have strong fingers

that will be

there

with you!

love is tough!

Just as you have been
there in <u>so</u> many

ways for so many
folks, including me.

We are a tapestry
of life that never
totally unravels !

and only gets
bigger!

dying has been a

 word

But in reality it is

a dyNAMic

And you
will !

SAFETY
RULES !

We know this with

every inhale

and exhale

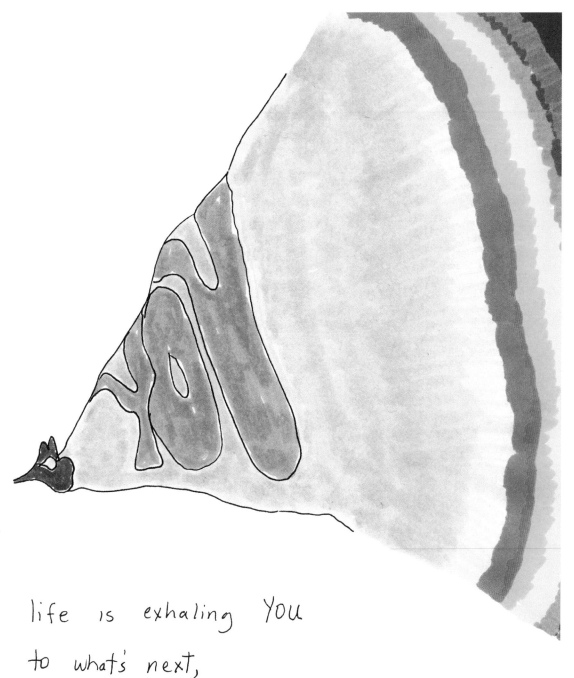

life is exhaling YOU
to what's next,
which is ALIVE!

my heart 🖤
loves
your heart 🖤

And that connection

is

A Bridge!

Up with Bridges!

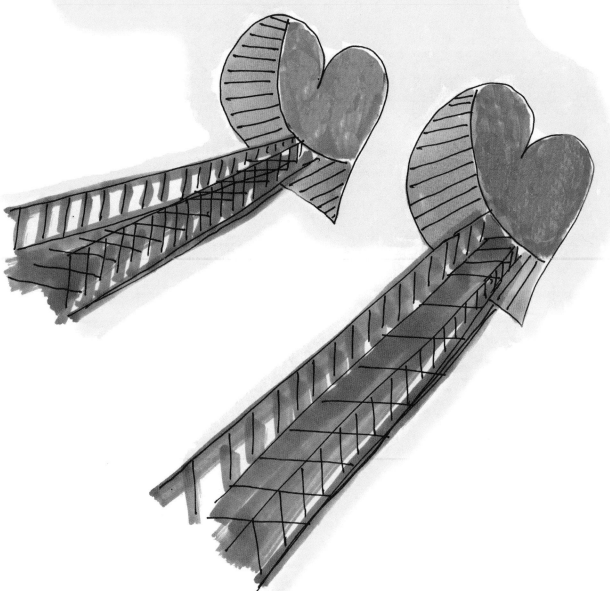

we   will   meet

again

we will love again + again.

You are completely loved, right now.

You are loved NOW + ALWAYS!

We love You.

_____

_____

_____

_____

_____

_____

friends + family sign here

Crossing the Bridge

~

Softening Transition

~

If you like Lindsey in print, you will love her forthcoming projects and classes!

Watch for upcoming webinars
Go to LindseyBerkson.com

Lindsey Berkson is a researcher and certified nutritionist; she has been an adjunct professor, educator of physicians for the application of nutrition in clinical practice, radio show host, health advocate for women, and author of numerous books. Lindsey Berkson is a participating scholar at a science driven think tank at Tulane and Xavier Universities (Center For Bioenvironmental Research). Berkson has faced many health challenges due to a drug exposure in utero, and has become a well-respected keynote speaker on motivation as well as health and science.

Berkson's books include: *Safe Hormones, Smart Women, Hormone Deception, Healthy Digestion the Natural Way, Natural Answers for Women's Health, My Mother Who Wore Her Purse as a Shoe, Why is it so hard to keep all your ducks in a row, Retraining the Tongue, Crossing the Bridge, Why Is Love So Hard?, Juicy Souls,* and *HeartSpeak.*

16997880R00031

Made in the USA
Lexington, KY
25 August 2012